D1455928

RANDY'S CORNER

DAY BY DAY WITH...

SHAKIRA

BY
TAMMY GAGNE

Mitchell Lane
PUBLISHERS

P.O. Box 196
Hockessin, Delaware 19707
Visit us on the web: www.mitchelllane.com

Mitchell Lane
PUBLISHERS

Printing   1   2   3   4   5   6   7   8   9

RANDY'S CORNER

DAY BY DAY WITH. . .

Library of Congress Cataloging-in-Publication Data
Gagne, Tammy.
Day by day with Shakira / by Tammy Gagne.
   pages cm. — (Randy's corner)
Includes bibliographical references and index.
ISBN 978-1-68020-107-9 (library bound)
1. Shakira—Juvenile literature. 2. Singers—Latin America—Biography—Juvenile literature. I. Title.
ML3930.S46G34 2014
782.42164'092—dc23
[B]
   2015017399

eBook ISBN: 978-1-68020-108-6

ABOUT THE AUTHOR: Tammy Gagne has written dozens of books for children, including *Adele* and *Ke$ha* for Mitchell Lane Publishers. She resides in northern New England with her husband and son. One of her favorite pastimes is visiting schools to speak to kids about the writing process.

SHAKIRA LAUNCHES HER FIRST COLLECTION OF BABY PRODUCTS WITH FISHER-PRICE.

Shakira has sold more than 70 million albums worldwide. This superstar doesn't just sing. She is also a loving mother, generous volunteer, and passionate advisor. Shakira has coached other promising singers on the hit television show, *The Voice.*

Shakira Isabel Mebarak Ripoll was born February 2, 1977, in Baranquilla, Colombia. She is the only child of Nidia Ripoll and William Mebarak Chadid. She has eight half-siblings from her father's earlier marriage.

SHAKIRA'S MOTHER SHOWS PHOTOGRAPHERS
A PICTURE OF SHAKIRA AT ONE YEAR OLD.
WHEN SHE WAS JUST A BABY, IT WAS CLEAR
THAT SHAKIRA WAS DIFFERENT. WHEN SHE
WAS EIGHTEEN MONTHS OLD, SHE KNEW HER
ALPHABET.

When she was quite young, one of Shakira's older brothers was killed in a motorcycle accident. At eight years old, she wrote her first song "Tus Gafas Oscuras" about the sunglasses her father wore while he mourned his son.

Shakira loved music and dancing even as a young girl. She first heard Arabic music and saw belly dancing when her father took her to a Middle Eastern restaurant. She connected with the culture and the music. Since it was part of her own heritage, it would one day become part of her musical style.

10

Shakira's family wasn't rich, but her parents made sure she knew that not everyone was as fortunate as they were. They once took her to a local park where homeless children lived. In 2009, she told *The Telegraph*, "That image of those kids that day in the park has never left my mind."

13

n Shakira was just 13, she landed ar
tion to perform for Sony Colombia
utives. They enjoyed her unique blen
ic, Latin, and rock music so much th
offered her a record deal. She was c
vay to becoming the best-selling
nbian musical artist of all time.

15

SHAKIRA
PLAYS
GUITAR.

16

In 1997, she decided to move to the United States to pursue an international music career. After settling in Miami, she began teaching herself to write songs in English. By 2002, she had the best-selling single of the year—"Whenever, Wherever."

In the years that followed, Shakira released several more albums. Each one was a huge success. She also won two Grammy Awards and two Latin Grammy Awards. She dedicated one of them to Colombia, adding that the war-torn nation "never forgets to smile."

2006 LATIN GRAMMY AWARDS

SHAKIRA
WON THE
2011 LATIN
RECORDING
ACADEMY'S
PERSON OF
THE YEAR
AWARD.

19

SHAKIRA PERFORMING AT THE 2014 FIFA WORLD CUP.

SHAKIRA PERFORMING AT THE 2006 FIFA WORLD CUP

In 2010, Shakira recorded the song "Waka Waka (This Time for Africa)." That same year it became the theme song for the FIFA World Cup. This wouldn't be her last link to football—soccer to her US fans. Her stage performance closed out the 2014 FIFA World Cup in Brazil.

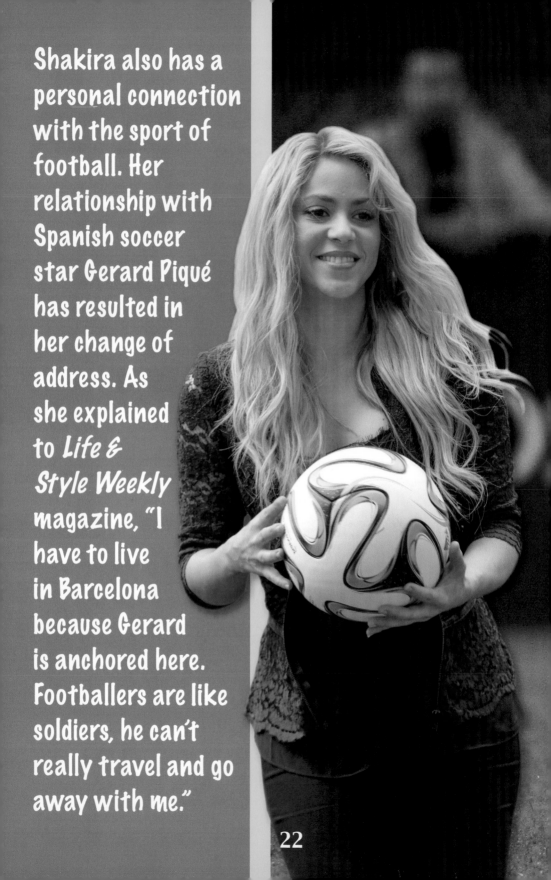

Shakira also has a personal connection with the sport of football. Her relationship with Spanish soccer star Gerard Piqué has resulted in her change of address. As she explained to *Life & Style Weekly* magazine, "I have to live in Barcelona because Gerard is anchored here. Footballers are like soldiers, he can't really travel and go away with me."

GERARD PIQUÉ FROM FC BARCELONA

23

GERARD'S MOTHER

SHAKIRA AND GERARD'S MOTHER ATTEND ONE OF HIS FOOTBALL MATCHES IN BARCELONA WITH MILAN AND SASHA.

In 2013, Shakira and Gerard welcomed a son. They named their baby boy Milan. Shakira wrote on her website, "The name Milan (pronounced MEE-lahn), means dear, loving and gracious in Slavic; in Ancient Roman, eager and laborious; and in Sanskrit, unification..." On January 29, 2015, the couple welcomed their second son, Sasha Piqué Mebarak.

Shakira appeared in seasons four and six of NBC's hit singing competition *The Voice*. Like everything else she does, she gave this role her all. In an interview with host Carson Daly, Shakira shared, "You put your heart and soul onto the flourishing careers of the contestants. You want them to do the best they can."

SHAKIRA IN LOS ANGELES WITH FELLOW COACHES ADAM LEVINE, USHER, AND BLAKE SHELTON IN 2013.

In addition to being a UNICEF Goodwill ambassador, Shakira also raises money for the Barefoot Foundation. This organization provides education, health, and nutrition services to families that cannot afford them. She truly never forgets those less fortunate than herself.

Whatever the future holds for the superstar, it will surely include giving back. In addition to her other charity work, Shakira has also built eight schools in Colombia, Haiti, and South Africa. She told *CBS Sunday Morning*, "I always felt that I could make a change, a difference, even if it was a small difference—I knew that I could do something, you know?"

SHAKIRA VISITS A POOR NEIGHBORHOOD OF HER COLOMBIAN HOME TOWN BARANQUILLA.

30

IN 2014, SHAKIRA DEDICATED A SCHOOL FROM HER FOUNDATION "PIES DESCALZOS" IN A NEIGHBORHOOD IN CARTAGENA, COLOMBIA.

FURTHER READING

FIND OUT MORE

Barefoot Foundation
http://www.fundacionpiesdescalzos.com/en/

Shakira (Official Website)
http://www.shakira.com/home

Shakira. Shakira. Milwaukee: Hal Leonard, 2014.

The Voice (Official Website)
http://www.nbc.com/the-voice

Williams, Zella. Shakira: Star Singer. New York: Powerkids Press, 2010.

WORKS CONSULTED

"Carson Daly Interviews Shakira: Talks New Music, Working with Rihanna, The Voice, & More!" 97.1 Amp Radio. February 19, 2014. http://amp.cbslocal.com/2014/02/19/carson-daly-interviews-shakira-talks-new-music-working-with-rihanna-the-voice-more/

Berns, Roberta M. *Child, Family, School Community: Support and Socialization.* Independence, KY: Cengage Learning, 2012.

Bibel, Sara. "Shakira Speaks With 'CBS Sunday Morning' About Building Schools for Underprivileged Children." *TV by the Numbers.* March 20, 2014. http://tvbythenumbers.zap2it.com/2014/03/20/shakira-speaks-with-cbs-sunday-morning-about-building-schools-for-underprivileged-children/246610/

Cooper, Diana. "Shakira COMPLETELY Wrapped Around Gerard Piqué's Finger, Says She's 'So Proud to Be a WAG.' " *Life & Style Weekly.* March 16, 2014. http://www.lifeandstylemag.com/posts/shakira-completely-wrapped-around-gerard-pique-s-finger-says-she-s-so-proud-to-be-a-wag-36111

Dadds, Kimberly. " 'Just like his father, baby Milan became a member of FC Barcelona at birth': Shakira announces happiness after son is born." *Daily Mail*, January 22, 2013. http://www.dailymail.co.uk/tvshowbiz/article-2266663/Shakira-gives-birth-baby-son-Milan.html

Paternostro, Silvana. "The Weekend Interview: Shakira's Colombian War." *Wall Street Journal*, April 3, 2010. http://www.wsj.com/articles/SB20001424052702304252704575156063289919070

Picoli, Sean. "Latin Grammys Air Two-language Special." *Sun Sentinel*, September 14, 2000. http://articles.sun-sentinel.com/2000-09-14/news/0009140202_1_latin-grammys-gloria-estefan-pop-album

"Shakira." BET.com. http://www.bet.com/topics/s/shakira.html

Smith, Julia Llewellyn. "Shakira Interview." *The Telegraph*, September 1, 2009. http://www.telegraph.co.uk/culture/music/rockandpopfeatures/6122146/Shakira-interview.html

INDEX